UNEXHAUSTED TIME

EMILY BERRY

Unexhausted Time

First published in 2022
by Faber & Faber Ltd
Bloomsbury House
74–77 Great Russell Street
London WC1B 3DA

Typeset by Hamish Ironside
Printed in the UK by TJ Books, Padstow, Cornwall

A CIP record for this book is available from the British Library

ISBN 978–0–571–37384–0

10 9 8 7 6 5 4 3 2

Contents

'Attempts at description are stupid,' George Eliot says, yet one may encounter a fragment of unexhausted time. Who can name its transactions, the sense that fell through us of untouchable wind, unknown effort – one black mane?

– Anne Carson, *Economy of the Unlost*

UNEXHAUSTED TIME

The gate stood open to let
her spirit out. Somewhere above,
a cacophony of seagulls. I told him,
I think they know when someone's died . . .
He laughed and said no. No, they don't.
This permanent kind of ceasing, like
a train slowly braking miles ahead
of the stop. I'm expecting something
and it feels like wearing a silk shirt . . .
Language incorrigible, same as hurt.

. . .

This story is a leaf that bursts out of
a branch, lives for a summer
and then dies. And it's your face striking
me like the time of an appointment I've
missed when I notice it after all this time.
I fear a catastrophe that has already occurred.
The communication always went wrong.
Like we were under a bad star. Bad?
The star was festering. Coldness around
all of my love. There was a woman
who stopped me in the street to shout
in my face about the violence she'd seen
in me. Brake lights in the early mist
like so many accusing eyes. *You did this.*
For a long time a man was dying,
making himself die, he couldn't stop,
and we forgot, we did our best to forget him.
How can a person walk in a shroud
all the miles of their life. But how
can they shrug it off. *We were searching
for a place of refuge for our love, but instead
the road led us to the land of the dead . . .*
I decided to try and write to you
about what I'm experiencing, since
I have no techniques for helping myself.
Why don't I have any techniques?
If you were on the other side you
might see the outline of my face
pressed against the veil, the look of
desperation. What if the deepest-rooted

dream of a tree is to walk, even just a little way?
A phobia is a ritual of not-doing. It did not
feel like a ritual but an injunction
from a distant regime, one we
forgot we'd voted for. It was a nice house,
quite plain and tasteful, but it had a bad
atmosphere. I don't like the way things
have turned out, but the law is the law.
It's interesting how the poet keeps saying
that life is full of grief, grief, grief.
A gate that leads to nowhere,
a tree cut short at the limbs,
nobody inside my dream . . .

. . .

Late summer. This ceaseless response.
Prolonged heat made me feel smudged.
It was not a bad feeling . . .
to be a smear on a windowpane . . .
light getting caught on me, then passing through.
The eras unfolded unblinkingly.
The past is our country: pawned,
broke down and unforgiveable, governed
by people we cannot trust, and we live in it.
Make me laugh and I will do anything.
Her face looking up at me with such a sweet
smile. Flushed from the drink or maybe the ride,
didn't I say it would be a long ride.
Her mouth glowing red and crisp
like the dying end of a cigarette,
not out yet. You always loved
the girl inside the boy, how that girl
can make a boy more boy, just like
the boy inside the girl can make her girler,
the way salt makes sugar sweeter . . .
She was like an old piano you only had
to tread past lightly for a key to ring out
in alarm. I too was an old piano . . .
I wanted to say, *Don't feel so much!*
But then I wanted to play a tune . . .

. . .

Funny you should mention a crow.
For years light . . . for years light eluded me
or stayed only a short time . . . something . . .
what was it . . . heavy in me . . .
a weight I couldn't put down . . .
How will you let her go,
the girl with the high ponytail
and all the wishes, the flooded
tremendous wishes . . . ?
In the valley there was a crystal shop
and, they said, a lot of healers.
At the top of the hill we lay beneath
the eaves trembling, serpentine
in one hand, labradorite in the other.
Earth star, base root, third eye.
Why then are we not healed?
We do not know the way home.
We relived all those days, days we
couldn't remember. We're trapped
between two worlds, we said.
We're trapped between two seasons.
How easily it gets flipped over and
we're on our backs, alone for ever,
staring at the smashed face of the moon.

. . .

In this house the white walls display
their scars, which are the stories
moths tell when I crush them to death
with my fingertip. The stories I make
them tell. The lonely angle of a lamp
and the books piled up beside the bed . . .
What can I do. What can I do to change.
I won't change. I won't change till the day I die.
Downstairs a baby's fury sounds eight,
nine times a day. Her parents break out into
the courtyard to weave the pram in circles
then go back inside. And the letterbox,
loose on its hinges, rattles all night
in the wind. How can I be less porous?
a friend wanted to know. Yes, how
can we keep our love from showing.
Should we keep our love from showing.
The intimacy is too much or it's not enough
and the soul, or whatever's in there,
yawns open for lack of reply.
Every life that touched mine so close
to the surface . . . your voice
coming out of my mouth . . .
I can't sleep and I can't eat and
one of those Mediterranean winds
with a special name blows through me.
Dawn awakening (no sunrise).
Birdsong at 5 a.m. . . . .

. . .

The boxes were there. To be opened any time . . .
I thought, should I go down that road again?
No. On balance not. A voice worn
all along its seams, I ought to stop
listening. I ought to stop.
The mind's self-deceptions inspire awe.
Its mountains. Must I walk there
alone, without a guide?
I do not know the things I know,
they are folded into my routines
imperceptibly. I do not see
what there is to be seen, the way
they tear the skin off an animal
and fit it to the human form.
Casualties of use. My index knuckle
hurts from tapping out my litany.
Maybe I should have asked for more . . .
but I was sealed up, like a package
that must be delivered whole,
or not at all . . . I mean,
so much happens in my mind,
it's almost enough . . . but not quite . . .
The last goodbye on a rotary telephone.
The pity I collected in my little cup.
When someone leaves you,
they flow out of you like milk,
and if you allow it, you can feed people . . .

. . .

It always seemed to me a kind of madness,
the gardens all in flower year after year.
But I suppose I was the mad one,
standing barefoot among the broken
crockery, shouting swear words
in an empty house. It was one of those
summers that yawned wider and wider
until I feared I might somehow fall out
of the world. Then it snapped shut
and the trees were bare, and the hammer
came down, and it rained nonstop
the day the votes were slipped hopelessly
into their boxes. The chain of command
delivering poison all the way down
from the top. I could not cross town
without sobbing, with a terrible sense
that I was being taken away. My face
twisted up from all those feelings.
I thought, in the middle of it I thought,
I don't have to finish this, I almost abandoned it,
but I went on. We waited hours to be seen,
and then we were turned away.

. . .

All statements purporting to be fact
are true. Nothing goes away . . .
You carry it with you,
if not on your back, or in your arms,
then somewhere behind your eye . . .
So be careful . . .
See the ghost scratching at the door frame
for the note that will free her.
The past is parked next to me like a dirty van
with messages fingered in the grime . . .
I drove it to a deserted forest
and left it there with busted tyres
but it came back . . .
It always comes back.
And there are new messages . . .

. . .

*This is the story of a man marked by an image
from childhood. Of a truth too fantastic to be believed
he retains the essential: an unreachable country,
a long way to go.* There is something shocking
about a family, the way they gather together,
all looking the same. The way they don't gather
together. At the back of the house the lawn
stretched out like a sheet, as if flung by the rockery.
There was a shed in which children conducted
business. There was a room with a frilled
counterpane. As a child I compiled lists of names
on long train journeys: Adelaide, Alice, Aline . . .
Why do you think I did that? Some letters
carried a sorrow they couldn't shake off, like *n*,
such a sad letter, always in the shadow of *m*.
I don't know why you care so much about
other people's poetry. Time would pool in corners
abominably. I mean the things they say. And I mean
the things other people say about other people's
poetry. *I am now so old. Most of what I read
doesn't interest me. The whole world is so prosaic.
Do you believe in omens? Of one thing I am absolutely
positive: there are certain things we cannot know.*
One day the shadows will take over the house,
and I will ask you, once and for all, to join me
in this firmament. I do not want to see myself
in another's image. Whose particularities become
a symbol. I could not see past my own voice.
Which will one day be still.

. . .

> 'Do you believe,' she went on, 'that the past dies?'
> 'Yes,' said Margaret. 'Yes, if the present cuts its throat.'
> – Leonora Carrington, 'Waiting'

One day you would say those words to her.
She looking up at you like a punished lamb.
The violent scene that upset him, and whose
meaning he was to grasp only years later. Your
father's unknown effort. I said to the saint,
Go back where you came from. I tried to burn
the relic to ashes but it would not catch. I took
to baking apple pies, your mother's only recipe.
The things a person does . . . how should we not
mind? The way they said she'd take the sacrament
like butter wouldn't melt. The way you said,
No amount of prayers will take away these sins.
Maybe she was afraid, and nobody would go to her.
Not now, not ever. All day and all night
the machine would stab its little needle.
Her with a tape around her neck, the radio
announcing deaths. The writer was wrong
when he said, *What one doesn't say doesn't exist*;
we've seen what doesn't exist. We've seen it
so much it might be better to have said it,
it's what is said that ceases to exist. *Do you hear*
his voice, still? Oh, I can, yes, I can, if you say that,
I can hear it in my head. A metaphor is a spell cast
to keep us away from the source. But we go on
lowering the bucket into the well. Afterwards,
perhaps, we don't feel so all alone. At what point,

I asked him, would he give up on fishing if he never got a bite? Oh . . . he said, a touch rueful, melancholy for his uncaught fish. Three stones lined up on the windowsill, a chipped saucer collecting rainwater. He laughed because it was as if he had made a promise to the fish, and he was that faithful. I would wait a long time.

. . .

My love was two pieces put together. It was,
but one day you could no longer feel the seam.
There must be something to say about the burning
weeks when the past came through like a hernia
and what could we do, what could we do.
The stillness in the house as I'm remembering.
It was a dream that would not get born. All night long.
As a child he sat in the car to get away from her.
He stayed out late with the stars and the hay bales.
Nothing sorts out memories from ordinary moments.
Later on they do claim remembrance when they show
their scars. Small fragments of life suspended in
everyday war. He hallucinated a door in the woods.
For maybe three seconds it hovered before him.
If he could only hold it – hold it there, oh, forever –
he'd be released. How is it the things that happen
to us seem to have happened already. I kept wondering
why you didn't call and if there was rainfall where
you were. When I was a small girl with wet sheets
and not a mother between us. But tell me, my love,
which other way should it be. I do believe the future
can influence the past. *All those little sounds add up*
and come together in a kind of hum. But it's so faint –
so very, very faint – you can't hear it unless you listen
carefully for a long time. I have seen poetry unleashed
by a single line, but I have not known where it got to,
the way a lure might be lost in a lake and the fish
still rise. I slipped the memento of the saint, your

mother's gift, under the door of the church. I sent those blessings back to their source and the devil take them, if you believe in the devil, which I do.

. . .

In a dimly lit room I practised saying
an awful thing. If she could stand it,
I would survive. I held my breath
and did not look. Your body like
a long stem. I am the flower.
I do not know if I have bloomed yet.
It was late, and over the city there
hung a perfect, unbearable glow.

. . .

Dream of a Dog

My life, and all our lives, I said sleepily,
so soft now, like the neck of a sleeping dog,
I lay my hand on it, as you have lain your hand
on mine (on my life), this tenderly, as the dog
noses deeper into sleep, as she sighs the way
a dreaming dog does, I wish my life was in
your dream, dog, I think it is, and she turns
onto her back so her stomach rises pale and
softly furred, and your words are travelling
through me, or, no, they travel over me, the
way a breeze makes fabric touch us, the fabric
of half-drawn curtains billowing from an open
window, as I pass and glance out on such
a day, the dog whimpering softly in sleep;
perhaps it's that you say I should have faith,
or that you have faith, in increments, while
my shoes are nosing through leaves and the
dog is alert or disappears (but she comes back),
if I had a dog she would be a kind of faith,
I would lift her onto my shoulder, the points
of her ears very elfin and her face, serious, tilted
to regard you, she would get down and run
and then, from a distance, up a slight incline,
when I call her, look back, then run on,
and I do believe in increments, as when
the dog brings me, in her dream, pine cones,
when she wriggles in my arms, her ribcage
strung like an archer's bow, when her paws
bend at the wrist in supplication, I do not see
the slow wheels in my blood turning, but

I ride them, I do not see what I know
and everything beneath that, which I may
come to know, or may not, the slow slow
discernment of the deep layer, air bubbles
rising from the dead zone, the dog in her
dream talismanic on a hilltop, the soft tips
of her ears in sleep, a slight sigh, all my life . . .

. . .

. . .

Nocturne

In some parts of the world children stay up late to see a new moon born, while I, for a long time, used to go to bed early, so I never saw the birth of a moon, but I witnessed many beheadings, in our country this is usual. I never saw a head that did not grow back, sometimes bigger than before, in this way our people disproved the laws of physics, how did this happen? No, I'm tired of your questions, we always wiped our blades and like I said, we used to go to bed early, for a long time.

Scholar

I had a close friend who was a scholar of unbelief. Once she interviewed me for her study and identified me as a believer in symbols. She had a designated category for this type of person, which I forget. I did not like to think of myself as belonging to a category. Yet I later encountered many other people who fell into it – they were often poets. For example, I set great store by the proverb about magpies. If I saw a single magpie it was not that I thought bad luck would befall me, but I saw the bird as symbolic of the sorrow that had blighted my life. It was a confirmation. Now the sorrow was accounted for, and it was beautiful, because magpies were. They had that deep indigo stripe among the black.

Mother

When my mother died I swore I would
remain sad for ever. But although some part
of me did remain sad, the larger part did not,
and I was forced instead to endure the guilt
I felt for again and again giving away pieces
of myself I'd insisted would never belong to
anybody else but her. I imagined trying to
explain this to some future incarnation ('Well,
but you were gone, what was I supposed to do,
I couldn't wait around indefinitely, I had to
look after myself . . .'), but none of my excuses
sounded remotely convincing and instead
I saw myself standing there in agony,
accepting my just punishment, which was
that eventually her fury and sense of
abandonment would overpower me and
become mine.

Baby

Once I saw a disturbed old woman coming out of a house with a baby. The baby was naked and being dragged along behind the woman. There was a used tampon attached to the baby somehow, it was caught on it or maybe it had got the string in its mouth. I didn't want to look too closely. I had a feeling that I had seen this woman and the baby before. The baby became disentangled from the woman, who wasn't paying much attention, and rolled out across the road. I ran after the baby and managed to grab it and hold it to my chest for comfort. It had a quite disgusting texture, damp and fibrous, not unlike the used tampon in fact. To the baby I whispered, *You're safe now.*

Snake

I went to visit André and for some reason I had a snake with me that I had to kill. It wasn't a lethal snake but its bites were very sore and itchy. Straight away I got bitten by the snake and after that I was chasing it around André's flat trying to kill it. The whole thing made me feel sick. André was able to relax and forget about the snake while we were talking but I was constantly on the lookout for the snake which was roaming free around the flat. It got under André's bed while we were sitting on it and I sprayed it several times with a mild detergent which hampered its progress slightly but was not enough to kill it. Finally I found myself bashing at its head with a ladle which eventually cut into its throat but it was a strange and repulsive process and I felt wretched about it.

Fish Tank

Once I watched a woman in a fish tank shitting directly into a tortoise's mouth. It was meant to be some kind of spectacle. She was invited to do it and was very happy to, and the tortoise was happy to eat.

Therapy

There were only two men in the therapy workshop. One was a young man from another country, whose means and modes of self-expression troubled the rest of the group, but we could not be sure to what extent this sense of trouble was prejudicial and based on our poor understanding of cultural mores which in this young man's country of origin were considered perfectly standard. He was always drawing up overflowing buckets from his deep wells of sadness and then dropping them back down again almost before anyone had got a glimpse of them. At least, that was our guess, because he generally maintained a deep, impermeable silence which had the queasy atmosphere of a lake that was so still as to appear to be a solid, or perhaps a gel, something sealed with a film, a film which – one had the impression – had formed due to the substance's fear of contamination through exposure to air.

Bird

I was making my way through the grounds of a stately home which had been turned into a public garden. I seemed to be being followed at a distance by a huge bird, like a heron, but pink, kind of coral-coloured. I felt like it was mimicking me. I hurried on to get away from it and saw a door into a small hut. I went inside thinking I would hide in there until the bird had gone away. The hut had windows at head height so I was able to look out and observe the bird's progress. I saw it approach another girl, who was with a man, probably her boyfriend. They were looking into some kind of display case. The girl was dancing, unaware of the bird, which was now right next to her. It started moving in time with her body, but slowly, as if insulting her. Then it turned in my direction. I ducked down below the window. There was a small bolt on the inside of the door but it didn't look strong. I worried that the bird would hear me locking it, so I held the door shut with my foot. When I heard breathing I knew the bird was right outside. I don't know how it got in. Its claws were like the claws of a giant insect, pink and reaching. There was one inside me. Deep. I was screaming. It was a very beautiful bird.

Ghosts (Homage to Burial)

A statistician would say: of all the millions of ghost stories ever told, what percentage would have to be true for ghosts to exist? The answer is that only one story would have to be true.

– Burial

You can invest everything in someone. This one feeling chopping you up. Anyone can go into the night. I just want to be gone. I want to be unknown. There's a storm coming. Euphoria trapped in a vial . . . I was once in these mountains, the middle of nowhere. I used to get taken away. A lot of things were wrong, cold things, bad things. The weight of the decisions in you. You'd see these fires. Someone upset on the other side of the world. It's like a ouija board, it's . . . the devil's face in their eyes, that feeling like a ghost touched you, like finding a body in a lift shaft on the other side of the night, even if you fight to see it, you'll never see anything. I love rain, safe haven. Deserts, forests, people. I just want to be a symbol you alone could hear. Someone in your head. Everyone knows those sorts of feelings. When there's nowhere to go, tearing through an empty building. The image of where you just were still on your retina. If you talk about it, it just sort of disappears . . .

House

We live in the house of a man who has committed suicide. He's going to do it again tonight at six o'clock. We have to live through it again in time. We've lost track of how many times. The first time it happened again we ran outside, we couldn't bear to live through it another time. Now when the gun goes off we don't even flinch. Other than that, nothing changes. We remember all the mistakes we made the first time, if they were mistakes. We make them again, every time, we think it might be different this time.

The Remains of the Day

I am lying in the foetal position on a beach in the east of England. Give me strength, I say to myself, absolutely literally. England does not exist. My enemies consider me a hard, angry and indispensable spirit and I do not blame them. How easy it is to do nothing, like a spider that has crawled up a wall and sits there on the ceiling. In late afternoon light I am counting your favours slowly like receipts. Imagination, morality, performance, farewells, spending, travel, war, needs, business, concession, feelings of entrapment and aloneness, no rescue. Please! Melancholic people are repugnant. I say to my detractors. The only way you will get any answers is by revealing something. And the air clings to me like a thick layer of menthol balm, trying to draw something out, some sickness. Who am I to claim a spider does nothing. I can't help noticing that my body appals you. Or is it my mind. Some combination of the two. And the tasks are mounting. When I regard a person with utter contempt, when I permit the disgust his lechery inspires to come to power inside me I know I will never allow him to see such a precious spectacle. May his weakness take hold of him like a suffocating vine. My country engulfs me. It is in a very bad state of repair, crowded with old furniture. The smell of refuse in the stairwell. Bad odours make me curious, but I am a tired woman. There is another shore, but it will never get here. Tell me how I should love you! They are rioting in the streets, they are feverish with injustice while my neck aches from studying a number of compelling thoughts. I am being observed, it transpires, from a distance by a huge coral-coloured bird. I may be paranoid, but I feel like it's mimicking my movements. How to escape. I told you don't come back, I said, and try to go to sleep. The only way to fall asleep is to forget about being awake, but I remember everything. I had noticed the vigour and enthusiasm with which the damned were depicted being drawn down into hell. And the choir of schoolgirls singing in the background, judgemental. Your stupid, beautiful face. I kept seeing these signs that warned of DEEP EXCAVATIONS. And I do not even know what it is you do to me. There is a bad thing in the mind that has not been digested, understand? This is why I have pain. My neck aches. And I am a very proud nation. The future like an insectile leg creeping over the rim of something – the horizon.

Paris

I went to Paris to visit a writer I admired. Because I was not confident he really wanted me to be there, he promised me that he did and we hugged for a long time but he let go first and I was not completely reassured. In his apartment he had taken my photograph when I had just finished showering and was looking rather dishevelled because I had dressed hurriedly and I asked if he would take another one later, or if maybe we could take a selfie together. He was very smartly dressed, he said he always dressed like this. I wondered if he would post the photo to his social media, as he sometimes did with other writers he had met, or if I wasn't famous or interesting enough. Then I wondered if I would post the photo to my own social media, either if he posted it, or if he didn't, because I didn't very often post such pictures, I didn't like the way they came across. I wanted to appear secure and aloof but it seemed to me that what such pictures conveyed was quite the opposite, even though that wasn't their intention. Actually it was partly this tendency that made me like this writer (who I liked so much without ever having, until now, met him, that I had dreams about hanging out with him in Paris), the idea of the insecurities that might lie behind his social media feed, which is to say his personality, as I imagined it, the traces of which, sensed digitally, had slid under my skin like a secret divulged only to me. This sense made me think that perhaps I should post the photo, because I wouldn't want him to think that I wasn't excited to meet him, or that I didn't want people to know we had met and been intimate enough to collaborate on such a photo, even if the posting of it revealed I did not feel secure in the collaboration. But I thought quite a lot of people probably would not pick up on this, being too preoccupied with their own insecurities, and after all what was there to cause me to feel insecure? He had done almost everything in his power to assure me that I had every reason to feel secure, except by going to such lengths that he himself would feel insecure in the event that I failed to assure him of his security.

Holes

In the midst of a continual programme of demolition and reconstruction, we noticed, one summer, that our city had begun to replicate, via its infrastructure, the prohibitions of the mind. There were roadworks constricting almost every major thoroughfare. Buses were regularly terminated short of their destination or treated passengers halfway through their journey to the wearying and ominous automated announcement, 'This bus is on diversion'. A number of these roadworks were connected to the development of a high-speed railway line whose viability had never been proven, now a pawn of warring factions of the government. Others looked temporary and unconvincing, as though they were only props intended to convey the impression of industry, but whether they were temporary or not, they remained. Our illusion of control, fundamental to whatever fragmentary sense of well-being we could cling to, became ever more illusory until it vanished completely. Several times I watched a man in a fluorescent vest roughly pry up a drain cover with a screwdriver, kneel down and start poking around inside it, something I took personally. You saw things like this every day in the city, where they were always digging. They would scratch and scratch with their tools at the surface of roads until they split them open because this was a necessary precursor to change, and change was intrinsic to growth. Anyone could see that the pursuit of perpetual growth was maniacal, but it went on all the same. Naturally the human body ceases to grow after a certain age; what grows after that are malignancies, like the *growths* one saw all over the city. It was unremarkable until you looked at it on the macro scale; in fact nothing ever changed, nothing of note, we had instead the sense that what was being uncovered in this relentless excavation was an advanced condition of sclerosis, a hardened and continually hardening rigidity, resistant to change. It was the same state we ourselves endured, were *made hard* by, in this city which had more and more holes where something had been dug up and never filled in (they could never be filled in, not really, even if they were filled in the city would still never be anything other than a collection of filled-in holes). On my route into town I passed buildings still standing that had been ripped half to pieces by bulldozers, looking desolate, bombed (though they had not of course been bombed, it had been arranged for all the bombing to happen elsewhere), their insides on show, like wrecked dolls' houses atop a trash heap.

Which is what they were, in a manner of speaking, to the forces of money that powered this city and destroyed it every day, except that they had not been cherished as a doll's house is often cherished, they had been blighted and abandoned even as they stood intact. Torn-off wiring stuck out all over these blasted buildings like hair standing on end, and your hair did stand on end to see the remains of so many rooms that once enclosed people, providing, in the best-case scenario perhaps, the illusion of safety and permanence, if not actual safety and permanence, which was elusive in this city, even in this city, which was said to be among the world's most important, this most powerful, most desirable, most influential, most visited, most expensive, innovative, sustainable, most, of course, investment-friendly, most popular for work city in the world.

Lip

We went to visit an old woman. She had recently lost a nephew or a grandson, I forget which. We were sitting at a table in the kitchen having tea, and the woman was lamenting that so many bits of her were falling off. I asked if there were any she could show us. She took hold of her lower lip, which I now saw was unattached to the rest of her face and just propped there against her mouth. She handed it to me on a plate. It did not look appetising. To oblige her I took my knife and fork, cut off a small piece and started chewing it. I chewed for a long time. I sat there smiling at the old woman, tormented, because now she had no lower lip, her bottom teeth were exposed as she spoke, all this and if my life depended on it I could not eat what she had given me.

Opinion

My friend reported that he had seen his therapist walking in a local park. His therapist had bad dress sense, he said, and seeing him in the wild like this only strengthened his opinion on the matter. He chose to wait behind a tree until his therapist had passed so that they would not have to encounter one another. But he could not be sure whether he did this to avoid the awkwardness that comes with meeting one's therapist in public, or rather because he could not bear anyone to see him talking to a person with such poor taste in clothes. In particular my friend was bothered by the therapist's shoes, which he described as 'embarrassing'. He felt he would have to tell his therapist, as soon as possible, how embarrassed he was by his shoes, even though it would probably hurt the man's feelings, otherwise the therapeutic alliance might be compromised.

Gods

While her companion talked on and on she aimed to keep her expression neutral but allowed her gaze to pass occasionally from his face to the large colourful painting behind him, which depicted a pair of Hindu gods cavorting in an idyllic landscape. Just to the right of his head she had a glimpse of a bright blue pool beneath some trees, and as she nodded and murmured small sounds of encouragement she imagined herself plunging into the lake and swimming with a powerful front crawl to the other side.

Bad Stone

One summer I bought a pale green stone
from a crystal shop, carefully selecting it
from a number of almost identical stones
because this one most attracted my
attention. I deliberately waited and watched
the stones, to see which one would call to
me. But shortly after I took the crystal home
I became convinced that it was possessed
by a bad energy. I believed the stone was
haunted. The bad energy was such that I
kept the stone hidden in a drawer for a long
time until I decided this was not effective and
brought it out again. I thought I could throw
it away, but I could not. I thought I could
cast it into a lake, or place it ceremoniously
somewhere in nature, such as in the lap of a
tree, or among pebbles at the edge of a stream,
where whatever was troubling the stone could
flow away into the earth. I thought I could
take it to a cemetery and set it on a significant
gravestone, or leave it on the steps of a church.
But I could not bring myself to do any of these
things. I learned that such stones could be
washed in the light of a full moon, and so I
placed it, one night, on a window ledge. The
full moon came and went and by all rights
the crystal should have been purified, but my
sense of its badness did not lessen, if anything
it got stronger, when I thought of the stone it
was a small burning place in my mind, either

so cold it was hot, or so hot it was cold, I was pierced by the stone the way mothers of newborn babies are said to be pierced by their cries. I left it in the spot where it had taken its full moon bath, and where it would go on to be bathed nightly at every stage of the moon's cycle for many months. During this time there were several storms and I began to hope that a strong gale would dislodge the stone and it would fall and be lost in the gardens below, never to be encountered again, that the impact of the fall might knock the badness out of it, that it would dissipate in air, but none of this happened, the stone stood firm. I hardly ever saw it, in its place on the window ledge it was outside, out of sight, at the furthest margins of my home, sometimes weeks would pass when I didn't think of it, but then, without warning, when I was brushing away a cobweb from the corner of the window frame, or wiping a wet cloth along the sill, I would catch sight of the stone through the glass, it was round and smooth and could fit perfectly in the centre of my palm, though I had not held it for a long time, possibly I would never hold it again, such was my fear of its badness. Increasingly the stone looked clouded, like an eye losing sight, and it had a faint grey vein becoming, I felt sure, more pronounced, as if it was old and tired of

enduring the dark nights and the squeaking of
bats and the cold and the rain and the moon's
relentless phases and its sanctimonious light
and my refusal to claim what belonged to me.

Empty

I received a message from a friend announcing that she was pregnant. She explained that she was going to die when the child was born, and would like to meet up with me before then. I thought of my own womb hanging empty inside me and was pierced with joy. I'm so sorry, I said, I'm busy.

Street

Walking along the street one afternoon I found myself abreast of another pedestrian who, for whatever reasons, perhaps the same as my own, could not bring themselves to generate a surge in pace sufficient to overtake me. So we continued in that way for some time, almost companionably, and when at last something did compel them to break away I felt a pact had been torn and I knew once and for all that my worst fears were true: I was all alone in the world and no one could save me.

Boat

The man I love and I are at sea in a small boat. We're in rough waters and there is a sense of unease. I look towards the horizon and see an immense, towering wave gathering force in the distance. Very soon it will reach our boat, and I know it will obliterate us. I turn to my beloved and embrace him desperately, telling him how much he has meant to me and how grateful I am for every minute we have spent together, even for these last painful but infinitely precious seconds, but he fails to appreciate the seriousness of the moment.

News

For a long time I experienced the quality of the dark in my city as something untrustworthy. When I went out in the evening it felt as though I were emerging in the dead of night or doing something profoundly at odds with the preferences of my body and mind. The warmth emanating from lit interiors did not comfort me but only reinforced my sense of alienation. I used to believe that if you write things down you can keep them away from you. So far this has not proved to be true. As my mind turns again and again through the possible panaceas or poultices I might apply to my psychic wound – hitherto impervious to every style of mind and body therapy you could care to name – I must contemplate the final truth that pain is indestructible and it is with a kind of relief that I recognise this epiphany, one I have had many times before and which never fails to seem like news to me.

. . .

This Spirit

This spirit she came upon me as I slept – in such a way
my life or yours could come to be so thoroughly owned –
she was reckless – I knew she would make me run away
with her – I said spirit, slow down – but the spirit wanted
to ride – but I am so afraid, I said – I have all this tenderness
to impart – but the tenderness is not mine to give away –
but all your tenderness is your own tenderness, said the spirit –
it is not, I said – why then did you give it all away? – I did
not give it away – then it is yours to give away – the spirit
riddled like this – if in her arms I read a story – if out of her
arms I had the choice to write one but I chose not – chose not
because I did not know where I was going – because my path
broke down & I had this choice – stay or split – if I knew that
were I to split one part of me would become a ghost – if I did
not know yet which part – if the voice calling me out asked me
to describe the splitting & I did – if I said it was like smoke
spiralling outwards – it was like smoke lifting off me taking on
form & leaving me – if it was like a delicate girl I never met
but dreamed of – if it was like the flags of my youth fluttering,
far out at sea – like breathing out a breath you will never take
back in – but you know you can never take any breath back in –
if I saw her outside of myself & mourned her like I have mourned
no other loss – if I knew it was both a miracle & the most terrible
tragedy – to open up – release a flame – watch the flame go –
have you seen it? A flame that can ride water – she was my
daughter & if I could I would send her to you, if I sent her to you
would you take her? Listen, I ran this out of me because I knew
it would burn me down – my trainers press the ground & lift up
again – I saw myself on my back in high grass in high summer
with everything coming to me – how this ghost left me & printed

a new person all over me – I could peel her off or live like this –
I cried – *one or both will destroy me!* – the spirit called it fate but
I knew it was just drama – *I will never know why a good person
must die* – fate does not exist I said, but every door I opened showed
YES YES YES – I shut each one & locked it – checked the locks
three times – went back & checked them again – shook them to be
sure – drew hearts round the keyholes so the spirit would know
I loved her – it wasn't – it was never – that I didn't love her –

after Nadia Reid

. . .

You trod your lonely path and I trod mine,
and no one would drink from my tap but me,
this water which wouldn't stop flowing.
Irrevocably, the born arrive, and they can't
be put back, no, but who on earth would want
to put them back. I reached a door, passed
through it, reached another door, and so it
went on, there was nobody at home to greet me.
Once I saw someone I thought I knew.
What if just under this layer of life you could
find the old one, moving forward just the same,
and just above, what's yet to come, would I
know myself if I met me now, coming the other
way back then? I couldn't think of any reason.
When she had something painful to tell, it was usually
her way to introduce it among a number of disjointed
particulars, as if it were a medicine that would
get a milder flavour by mixing. I've been watching
a tall thin tree bending over and back
in the wind. Mamma mia, how can anyone bend
so much without breaking? I said I had been lost
in a fantasy world in which I could travel freely.
She said the fantasy world was this one.
At the hour of my death I did not die,
but was born again in this life.

. . .

A faint whisper of contagion, then a cloud.
Everything in the diary crossed out.

. . .

For a number of months I had observed
astonishing quantities of rain. Spring rain,
summer rain, autumn rain. *The sound of
heavy winter rain.* It was a strange time
and I loved to go to sleep, I loved to go
to the top of the hill in the pale light
of dawn and think back to the world
I knew. *Small fragments of war suspended
in everyday life.* An unfathomable cessation
of industry. On our street there were
saplings supported by stakes so they would
not lean, yet some, nonetheless, leaned.
Everyone was small and touched with light.
*I took the measure of the unbearable vanity
of the West, that has never ceased to privilege being
over non-being, what is spoken to what is unsaid.*
A feeling was named and I was sorry then
to have lost its magic unknownness,
the way it would come to mind like a
remembered secret and then slip away . . .
One day my therapist told me we were finished,
our sessions could come to an end. I protested
that I wasn't ready, I still needed more help,
please, I begged her, but she was insistent
and even radiant with the news. I was cured
and I would not need to come again.

. . .

To write a poem you must fall in love . . .
I did it many times. Beneath the trees
through which I walked in tears,
in wet school uniform. Tonight
the two dimensions of his face
will stare at her forever. I would fall
through a tear in time to get there,
I would fall through a tear in the story.
I had what I had, and it was never enough.
I didn't know and I didn't know.
The wind riffles through the chapters
of my life and something incurable and sad
starts up like a nineteen-year-old rain . . .

. . .

I felt I was born in a time when a lot of stuff
was just . . . not known . . . So we asked,
what was it like, to be a human being . . . ?
The clouds flushed with their
ridiculous secret, light.
Our minds like a playing field in spring . . .
Most feelings are very old, they have
been under the earth and then up
to the surface again, they have been
in the vapour of clouds and all across
the surface of the sky like hairline cracks
in the glaze on porcelain, our motivations
under the river like pebbles or like the lives
of unseen creatures that keep us alive . . .
There was a song we had never heard before,
it was a very old song, it was a song
we once knew but an imaginary one.
Listening to it was like looking at the sky
at a certain time of day, on certain days,
in midsummer, as it slowly pulls itself apart.
There were so many times I wanted to give up
but then a message would appear
from a complete stranger, from miles away,
telling me to go on. So I went on.

. . .

In my dreams they're all me . . .
even the man driving who's
staring straight ahead.
The arches of my feet ache
and when the wave hits the car,
it's me who's dying,
and it's me who's dying . . .

. . .

I agree, sometimes there is a soft core
of rot inside everything. But the poem
was blood temperature, and getting
hotter. In the dream I wore a yellow
raincoat and searched all the exits.
To the policeman, who knew, we swore
he would never leave without an explanation.
Now I try to notice the way a bird hops off
a branch into air. *For death, as an independent
power, is a lustful power, whose vicious attraction
is strong indeed.* I am done with your dying.
When you are gone I will not read what
you had to say. Tell it to me now, with breath
instead of ink. So I do not have to raise the dead.
If I could say this more viciously I would.
You are not one person. We would breathe
your ashes back into ourselves, which were
part of us already. We would breathe out
wildfire at each end of the opposable universe,
and yes, I accuse you of not loving yourself.
It's true there are passages in our minds
we have never been down. When you
are gone you are not gone. What grows
after fire is nurtured by disaster. Friend,
I would kill you for not wanting to live.
At the end of the world I would remember you
the way a tree remembers, reaching down
into the earth for messages. I would mark
your final gestures in disordered time

so that I could be waiting on the shore
for your return, so that the end
could come at the beginning.

after Johnny Flynn

. . .

The night prints itself upon me and I cannot
decide yet, whether to come to you whole,
or wait until I am gone. The end of the bed
shrouded in fog, thoughts touching my face
like soft rain. I must content myself with such
perfect things as these: traces of disorder,
burning couplets, very fierce inspiration . . .
Slept continuously for three days and nights,
like every true mystic. My voice falling over
the threshold like light. But you can't come in.

. . .

On the screen the spiritual adviser advised.
Someone told him they feared the world was
ending. Sure, he said, amused, but not today.
Get comfortable with death, he said, for we are all
dying. You want something permanent? he said.
There you have death, the only permanence.
And what happens in the land of the dead?
Oh, darling, nothing, nothing as far as I know.
And do they have money there?
Money in the land of the dead? They have no money.
Then how do they live?
Darling, nobody lives in the land of the dead.
The past did not unfold as we remember it.
What's gonna change? the mother said to her child.
What's gonna change? Nothing's gonna change,
so you better stop crying. Nothing's gonna change.
I saw trees yellow with happiness at the pinnacle
of their transformation. I saw light unfold the city,
which was a kind of benediction; not mine.
I learned we were seeds waiting in the soil
and we should not be afraid. It's true I have
lain in the dark and felt something give way.
I pressed my forehead to the earth and pictured
what they said, all the bad years pouring out
of me. I too can be an empty vessel, I can
change, I can change. Oh, once I was a seed
but when my shell split open I pinched
the tiny sprout until it withered away . . .

. . .

Nobody cares about one's personal trials and griefs . . .
One's trials and griefs are boring.
                                    – Katharine Kilalea, *OK, Mr Field*

What about personal relationships? the interviewer
said. *Your mother was furious.* The night feels
solid, like a block, indivisible. It could be any
time of day at all. *No, no,* you told him, *love
and understanding have nothing to do with each other.*
When you hate someone you must try even
harder to understand them. She sat in the room
sewing all night after what she'd done and didn't
say a word. Or she lay on the bed, dead, surrounded
by pill bottles. Classical music. Or she was dying
in pain for months and she couldn't give it up,
her anger, so her children took it from her and
choked on it for years. Or she had a father whose
mind was smashed by war like the city he smashed
to bits from the air. Or he worked every day
of his life till his bones wouldn't hold him up
and this was the thanks he got. Why should
anybody care about your sadness, about you not
getting what you want, how your eyes cloud over
with compromises. We had to take the money
out of your mouth in order to feed ourselves.
We had to destroy the village to save the village.
That's how it feels to see something offered
with one hand, taken away with the other.
The fountain so heavy with wishes they clogged
the drain. When the spoils of my life are delivered,

they will not be delivered to you. *The thing is,*
when we have the feeling that we are forced to change,
then it's going to be, that's my opinion, the wrong way.
The trick is not to force it and do it in a very clever way,
that you change without noticing, that would be the
perfect way. And love has nothing to do with it.

after Édouard Louis

. . .

I will tell you in detail what is affecting me.
How in their abundance words can seem
quite desolate. The night terribly dark
and the dawn broken open. The skin on
your face that covers over the bones . . .
It suddenly occurred to me that there
were bones. I did not even know what
I wanted, so many things at once, incompatible . . .
It would need to be someone who could
hear what you had to say. It would need
to be someone who could bear it . . .
To sit on the stairs in the dark without
complaint, to wait, and then go, and
come back again, and wait, that was love.
All our past lives and psychic debris bumped up
against the dock. *The memory of a twice-lived
fragment of time* . . . And your eyes are a song,
a song that is lost and will never be sung.
Writing was a mist rising off my life, that's all,
dependent on atmospheric conditions for its
existence. There was a time when I sensed this
chance mist all around me and I felt myself
beatified. I called myself angel of the mist . . .

. . .

What we do not possess belongs to us.
    – Fleur Jaeggy, *Proleterka*, tr. Alastair McEwen

Late spring evening, air smudgy with pollen
and barbecue smoke . . . I could have been
some effervescence caught in the light,
particles streaming out of me . . .
And I could have been the offspring
of a magic reaction where two points
come together, like the intersection of a cross,
or cycling under a bridge the moment a train
passes over it, like signing the text with an *x*.
I thought it was you withholding something,
but was it me . . . ? I was trying to catch hold
of this gorgeous tiny black fish that swam
vertically, like a seahorse . . . Thought it was
maybe a tadpole that would turn into a frog.
This feeling . . . something sweet and sharp in it,
like sugar and burnt oranges . . . like a felt-tip
across my lungs . . . I can't see your inwardness,
but I know the shape of it . . . The star inside of
yourself, I thought I saw its points tonight.
Months from now, high up by the reservoir,
the grass baked yellow as a cornfield, I felt it
moving in me, something like medicine, a slow
chemical my body made. I do not know if it
matters what is mine, and what is not mine.
I remember a clear lake with a pebble bed
5,000 miles away. A couple in white gowns
hanging paintings. Her face when she was happy.

It is something to see a heron in sunlight,
or the way a duckling stands and stretches itself
tall. There is no other life, but there are so
many lives. I felt certain you could rescue me
and so I never asked. If we can dream another
time, then we can find a way to live in it.
I'm a voice in the desert. About love. Thank you
for rescuing me with your words.

. . .

Light stretching my late summer shadow long
over parched grass, low sun, this alive, this
evening. Light of mid-morning picking out
all the trees' capillaries, black against the light
of blue's possibilities, would I rush outside
to see this, yes I would, this light? It's so kind,
it remembers me. Light of first thing, spilled sky
mixing day up, all the colours that go into day,
you wouldn't believe how many. Hard light
to be walked into like a mirror, day coming
down hard on its sharp edge; you can never
really see yourself the way others do, that's
the hard thing; or is it a good thing? (God
doesn't answer prayers, people do.) Light as
sunbeams that lie on the floor of your room
like ways through, they're not real ways
through they're just a reminder that there
may be a way through. See how the cat
anoints herself in the sunbeam, for she knows
she is not mortal and is waiting for the sign . . .

. . .

It was as if I were asleep the whole of my life
and I didn't know a thing, nothing on the
inside, not that life was life, or death is death,
how I was right or how I was wrong, that
nothing lasts and there's no one to blame, and
nobody gets out of it, not even you, not even
me, nobody gets out of it alive, but as long as
I live, come to me, as long as my love has the
strength of the blood that gives life and the
grief of the blood that drains away, come to
me wired and wild like the bare tree and the
shedding sky . . .

after Mary Oliver
& Tina Turner

. . .

No Name

What can I tell you? It was a summer that seemed to be
making history – their personal history – almost before
it began, and they stood back slightly, still in it, but
observing it, saying 'the summer this', 'the summer that'
all the while it was going on. They became obsessed with
a fountain, for example, one they walked past each day,
how abundantly it would reach upwards and yet be pouring
back down itself the whole time – all winter this fountain
had been dry, not saying a word. What more can I tell you?
Oh, everything – like how they would walk home in
the evenings when the light was soft, anything bad sliding
off them, and they would feel owned, completely owned,
in a good way, by the air, which would touch them constantly,
sometimes urgently, sometimes lightly, just to let them know
it was there, and they would think maybe this is what being
alive is, when they saw how complicated a tree was and how
it wanted them looking at it and saying this, how the colour
of a particular flower at this particular moment was redder
even than the life force, whatever that is, if you could open
it up and get right down inside it, if you could put your mouth
to it and become as red as that rose even, it was still redder
than that, and they wouldn't know what to do with themselves
so they wouldn't do anything except listen to the songs in their
heads which were sad ones like nearly all good songs and watch
this feeling rolling in, sunshine or rain, we don't know yet,
it's a good one, it's the best one, though it has no name.

. . .

Notes

The poems in this collection borrow and/or paraphrase material (indicated in the text by italics) from the following sources: p. 4: *The Color of Pomegranates* (dir. Sergei Parajanov, 1969) (subtitles); p. 7: Bobby Parker, IG message to the author; p. 10: Joan Didion speaking in *The Center Will Not Hold* (dir. Griffin Dunne, 2017); p. 12: *La Jetée* (dir. Chris Marker, 1962) (subtitles); Sigmund Freud, tr. Tania and James Stern, *Letters of Sigmund Freud, 1873–1939*, ed. Ernst L. Freud (1960); p. 13: *La Jetée* (dir. Chris Marker, 1962) (subtitles); Javier Marías, tr. Margaret Jull Costa, *A Heart So White* (1995); Elizabeth Chatwin speaking in *Nomad: In the Footsteps of Bruce Chatwin* (dir. Werner Herzog, 2019); p. 15: *La Jetée* (dir. Chris Marker, 1962) (subtitles); Richard Yates, 'Oh, Joseph, I'm So Tired' in *Collected Stories* (2008); p. 31: Burial interviewed by Mark Fisher in *Wired* (issue 286, December 2007) (the entire poem is a collage of Burial's words); p. 55: George Eliot, *Middlemarch* (1871); p. 57: Sarah Kane, *Blasted* (1995); *Sans Soleil* (dir. Chris Marker, 1983) (subtitles); p. 59: Sharon Olds speaking on the *Commonplace* podcast (episode 38, 4 October 2017); Jacqui Kenny, email to the author; p. 61: Thomas Mann, tr. H. T. Lowe-Porter, *The Magic Mountain* (1927); p. 65: Édouard Louis and Stephen Sackur speaking on *HARDtalk* (1 September 2019); *This American Life*, episode 684: 'Burn It Down' (27 September 2019); p. 67: Sigmund Freud, tr. Tania and James Stern, *Letters of Sigmund Freud, 1873–1939*, ed. Ernst L. Freud (1960); *La Jetée* (dir. Chris Marker, 1962) (subtitles); p. 69: Sarah Kane, *Crave* (1998). The book's epigraph is taken from *Economy of the Unlost (Reading Simonides of Keos with Paul Celan)* by Anne Carson, and is reproduced by permission of Princeton University Press. The epigraph on p. 65 is taken from *OK, Mr Field* by Katharine Kilalea, and is reproduced by permission of Faber & Faber and United Agents. The epigraph on p. 68 is taken from *Proleterka* by Fleur Jaeggy, tr. Alastair McEwen, and is reproduced by permission of And Other Stories.

Acknowledgements

Some of these poems (or earlier versions of them) previously appeared in *Bristol: A Poetic City*, *Granta*, *London Review of Books*, *New York Review of Books*, *Poetry* and *Prototype*; some were also included in my lyric essay 'The Secret Country of Her Mind', part of the artist's book *Many Nights* by Jacqui Kenny. I am grateful to Arts Council England and the Society of Authors for grants that supported my writing, to the book's first readers and to my editor and agent. Thank you to the friends who let me borrow from their lives and/or dreams. Thank you to all my loved ones, for everything.